Earth's Precious Resources

Soil

A resource our world depends on

Ian Graham

www.heinemann.co.uk/library

Visit our website to find out more information about **Heinemann Library** books.

To order:

 Phone 44 (0) 1865 888066

 Send a fax to 44 (0) 1865 314091

 Visit the Heinemann Bookshop at www.heinemann.co.uk/library to browse our catalogue and order online.

First published in Great Britain by
Heinemann Library, Halley Court,
Jordan Hill, Oxford OX2 8EJ, part of Harcourt
Education.
Heinemann is a registered trademark of
Harcourt Education Ltd.

Editorial: Andrew Farrow and Dan Nunn
Design: David Poole and Paul Myerscough
Picture Research: Melissa Allison and
Andrea Sadler
Production: Duncan Gilbert

Originated by Ambassador Litho Ltd
Printed in China by WKT Company Limited

ISBN 0 431 11554 0
08 07 06 05 04
10 9 8 7 6 5 4 3 2 1

British Library Cataloguing in Publication Data

Graham, Ian
  Soil: a resource our world depends on. –
  (Earth's precious resources)
  1. Soils – Juvenile literature
  I. Title
  552.5
A full catalogue record for this book is
available from the British Library.

Acknowledgements

The publishers would like to thank the
following for permission to reproduce
photographs: Corbis pp. **21** (Robert Holmes),
22 (Niall Benvie), **28** (Arthur Rothstein);
Ecoscene pp. **8** (Christine Osborne), **19**
(Robert Nichol), **20 top** (Alexandra Jones),
23 (Nick Hawkes), **29** (Sea Spring Photos);
FLPA pp. **4** (E & D Hosking), **10** (E & D
Hosking), **11 top** (E & D Hosking), **11
bottom** (B. Borrell), **12** (E & D Hosking),
24 (Derek Middleton); John Lewis Partnership
and Jasper Conran p. **15**; NHPA pp. **6**
(Stephen Dalton), **13**; PA Photos p. **27**; QA
Photos p. **20 bottom**; Science Photo Library
pp. **7** (John Mead), **18** (Peter Arnold
Inc./Volker Steger); TBG p. **25** (Daniel
Thistlethwaite); Topham Picturepoint pp. **14
top** (The British Musuem), **14 bottom**, **17**,
26 (ImageWorks).

Cover photograph reproduced with
permission of Holt Studios.

Every effort has been made to contact
copyright holders of any material reproduced
in this book. Any omissions will be rectified
in subsequent printings if notice is given to
the publishers.

The paper used to print this book comes from
sustainable resources.

Contents

Any words appearing in the text in bold, like this, are explained in the Glossary.

What is soil?

Soil is one of the Earth's many natural resources. We sometimes call it earth, dirt or mud. It is the top layer of the land. It is the natural material that grass, trees, crops and other plants grow in. Soil may be anything from just a few centimetres deep to many metres deep.

What is soil made from?

Soil is made from a mixture of sand, small gritty pieces of rock, water and dead plant material called **humus**. The amounts of the different materials in soil vary from place to place. These materials stick to each other and act like a sponge, soaking up water. The water in soil contains natural chemicals. Some of these are taken up by plants and used as food. These substances are called **nutrients**. People need some of these substances too. We get them by eating plants, or animals that eat plants.

Soil is important for growing plants, including the vegetables, fruit and cereals such as wheat, that we eat.

What is under the surface?

Soil is not the same all the way through. From the top down, it is divided into layers. These are:

- the litter zone
- topsoil
- subsoil.

The **litter zone** is made of leaves and other bits of plants that have fallen on the ground. They slowly break down and form humus. Below that, there is the topsoil. At the top, it is dark, crumbly and spongy, a mixture of grit and humus. There is air and water in the spaces between the grit and humus. Deeper down, topsoil contains less humus. The weight of the soil above squashes the **particles** closer together, so there is less air too. Below the topsoil, there is the subsoil. The subsoil is even more squashed down and contains very little humus or nutrients.

litter zone

topsoil

subsoil

rock

Soil is divided into layers. The topsoil contains the most humus and nutrients.

What else does soil contain?

As well as sand, grit, humus, water and air, soil also contains living things. Most of them are so small that you cannot see them! The smallest are bacteria and microscopic algae (simple green plants without stems, roots or leaves). These are living cells less than one thousandth of a millimetre across. Next come tiny animals – mostly worms, called nematodes, and creatures called tardigrades. Tardigrades are also called water bears, because they look a bit like tiny bears. Water bears are not bears at all. They are eight-legged creatures less than one millimetre long. They live in the water between the soil particles. Bigger earthworms crawl through the topsoil. Slugs, snails, insects and other creatures live in the cracks in the soil's surface.

Did you know?

There are more bacteria in a handful of soil than there are people on Earth!

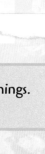

Healthy soil is full of living things.

Where does soil come from?

The raw materials for soil are being made all the time. Big rocks are continually being worn down into smaller **particles**. This can happen because **earthquakes**, **volcanoes**, **rock-falls** and **landslides** break pieces off large rocks. If water gets into cracks in rock and freezes, it expands, and pieces of rock break off. All of these natural processes wear rock down and produce the tiny particles that help to make soil. Plants die or shed their leaves. **Microbes** and **fungi** break down the dead plant material to produce **humus**. Wind blows the rock particles and dead plant material around until they settle somewhere. Plants grow into them, binding them together with their roots and forming new soil.

Rocks in rivers are rounded because water moves them around and bangs them into each other, wearing down the sharp corners. The small pieces that are broken off help to form new soil.

How can floods improve soil?

We usually think of floods as bad things, but people in parts of the ancient world sometimes relied on floods to grow crops to eat. When rivers flood, they spread mud on the land. The mud is rich in **organic** material. As this rots, it breaks down into simple substances that plants can take up through their roots and use as food.

In some places, farmers still rely on mud from floods to enrich their soil. Frequent floods in Bangladesh cause great hardship to the people who live there, but the river mud they spread over the land also improves the soil. This enables farmers in Bangladesh to grow up to three crops in one year.

This farmer is tending his crops by the River Nile, in Egypt. Farmers in ancient Egypt relied on the River Nile flooding to improve the sandy soil. It flooded almost every year, spreading mud onto the desert on each side of the river. This made the soil there more **fertile**.

What are the different types of soil?

Soil is not all the same everywhere. It depends on the raw materials that nature provides and the amounts of these raw materials differ from place to place. The main types of soil are:

- sandy
- clay
- chalky
- peaty
- loam.

Sandy soil

Sandy soil has lots of sand in it. The extra sand lets water drain through easily, so it dries out quickly after rain.

Clay soil

Clay soil has lots of very small rock **particles**. They pack together so tightly that they make the soil very heavy and sticky. If clay dries out, it becomes as hard as stone.

Every country is covered with a patchwork of different types of soils. In this map of Australia, each colour represents a different type of soil.

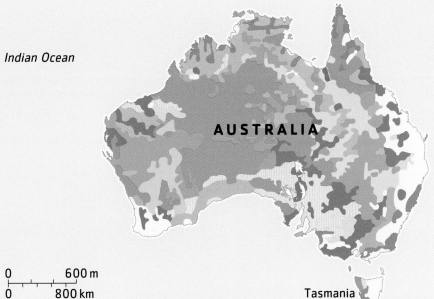

Indian Ocean

AUSTRALIA

Pacific Ocean

```
0          600 m
|---+---+---|
0          800 km
```

Tasmania

Chalky soil

Chalky soil has pieces of **limestone**, or chalk, in it. It is a bit like sandy soil and a bit like clay soil. Like sandy soil, water drains through very quickly. Like clay soil, it can sometimes be sticky and hard to dig.

Peaty soil

Peaty soil contains a lot of dead plant material. It is found in places where the soil is waterlogged, such as bogs. Peaty soil soaks up a lot of water like a sponge. Peat bogs grow very slowly, only about one millimetre every year. Digging out peat can destroy a peat bog and its special **habitat** for plants and animals. Taking peat from nature is strictly controlled by law to protect peat bogs.

Peat dug out of the ground like this can be dried and burned like coal.

Loam

The best soil for growing most plants is called loam. Loam is a spongy mixture of sand, grit, clay and **humus**. It doesn't dry out too quickly and it doesn't become waterlogged. It holds the right amount of water, air and **nutrients** for most plants.

How do plants and animals use soil?

Soil is essential for most of the plant and animal life on land. Plants take up water and **nutrients** from the soil and use them for growth. People and other animals take in these nutrients themselves when they eat plants.

Most people eat meat too. Our supply of meat also depends on plants, because the animals our meat comes from eat plants. Another way to say this is that our food chain begins with plants, and plants depend on soil.

Lots of animals make their homes in soil – from tiny creatures such as worms, spiders and ants, to larger creatures such as moles, rats, rabbits, foxes and badgers. Some ants make amazingly complicated homes in the ground, where thousands of ants live together.

Rabbits live in burrows that go deep into the ground.

Ants like these live in large colonies (groups) in the ground.

How do birds use soil?

Most birds build nests from the leaves, twigs, feathers and other materials they find in the soil's **litter zone**. Some birds, including swallows, use the soil itself to build their homes. They pick up muddy soil in their beaks and make mud nests. The nests are often stuck to trees, cliffs and buildings. Many birds swallow grit and **gravel** and use them to grind up their food. Some parrots in South America use clay soil in a very strange way. They eat it! They need it because the clay absorbs (takes in) poison from the fruits and seeds the birds eat. Some medicines made to treat people with tummy trouble contain the same type of clay, called kaolin.

Some birds build nests from mud.

Why is soil important to reptiles?

Scaly-skinned animals, such as snakes, turtles, lizards and crocodiles, are called reptiles. Most reptiles lay eggs and some build nests for their eggs. The Nile crocodile digs a hole in the ground, lays her eggs in it and then fills in the hole with soil. Other types of crocodiles and alligators pile up soil, mud and plants and lay their eggs in the middle of it.

Why are there worms in soil?

Worms not only live in soil, they also find all their food in it. As earthworms move through the ground, they take in soil. They keep anything they can eat and let the rest pass out of their body. Worms are good for soil, because they carry **organic** material down from the surface and mix the soil up.

Did you know?

Healthy soil is full of worms of all sizes. Earthworms take in their own weight of soil every day.

What do we use soil for?

People have used soil for thousands of years. They piled it up to make banks to mark out their land and defend their homes. They used it for growing plants to eat and to feed their animals. They also used clay soil to make bricks, pots and bowls. And they mixed coloured soils with water to make paints to decorate their bodies. Soil and the materials it contains are still used to do many of these things today.

People have been making pottery from clay for about 10,000 years. This vase was made by the Romans in the 2nd century AD.

What is Offa's Dyke?

Offa was a king in England more than 1200 years ago. To separate his kingdom from the Welsh lands to the west, he ordered a great bank of soil to be built. It stretched across the countryside for 270 kilometres (167 miles). It was up to 18 metres (60 feet) high. Another name for a bank of soil is a dyke, so it was called Offa's Dyke.

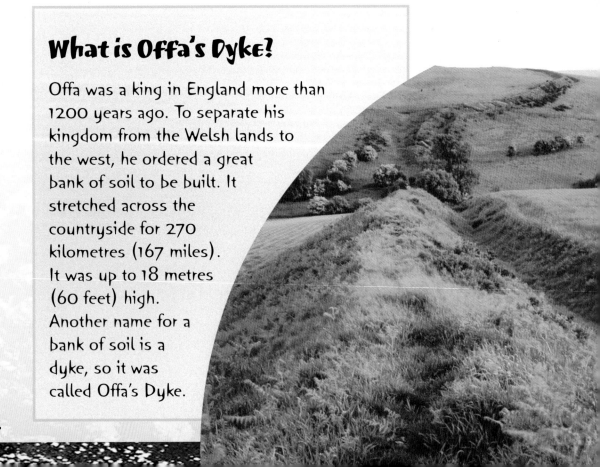

How is soil used in the home?

Some of the things we use every day, including plates and cups, are made from clay. There are different types of clay. The finest cups and plates are made from clay with the smallest **particles**. This is called china clay. It starts off as a soft white powder. When it is mixed with water, it sticks together and can be moulded into a shape. It is then heated to more than 1000 °C (1800 °F) so that some of it melts and changes to glass. This makes the clay hard and waterproof. Clay is also used in the production of rubber, paint, ink, paper and some make-up.

Did you know?

The largest particles in china clay – used to make the finest crockery, like this – are only about one hundredth of a millimetre across.

How is soil used to make new land?

Parts of some coastlines are washed away by the waves. But land does not have to be lost to the sea forever. The Dutch people have turned an enormous area of sea around the Netherlands' coast back into dry land. More than one-sixth of their country was once under the sea!

The Dutch **reclaimed** each piece of land by building a bank of soil around it. Then the water was taken out, leaving dry land. At first, this was done by hand. Then windmills were used to pump the water out. Now, the latest digging and pumping machines are used. Today, the low-lying parts of the Netherlands are protected by 3000 kilometres (1800 miles) of sand dunes and earth banks, or dykes.

Did you know?

Nearly two-thirds of the people in the Netherlands live on land that is below sea level!

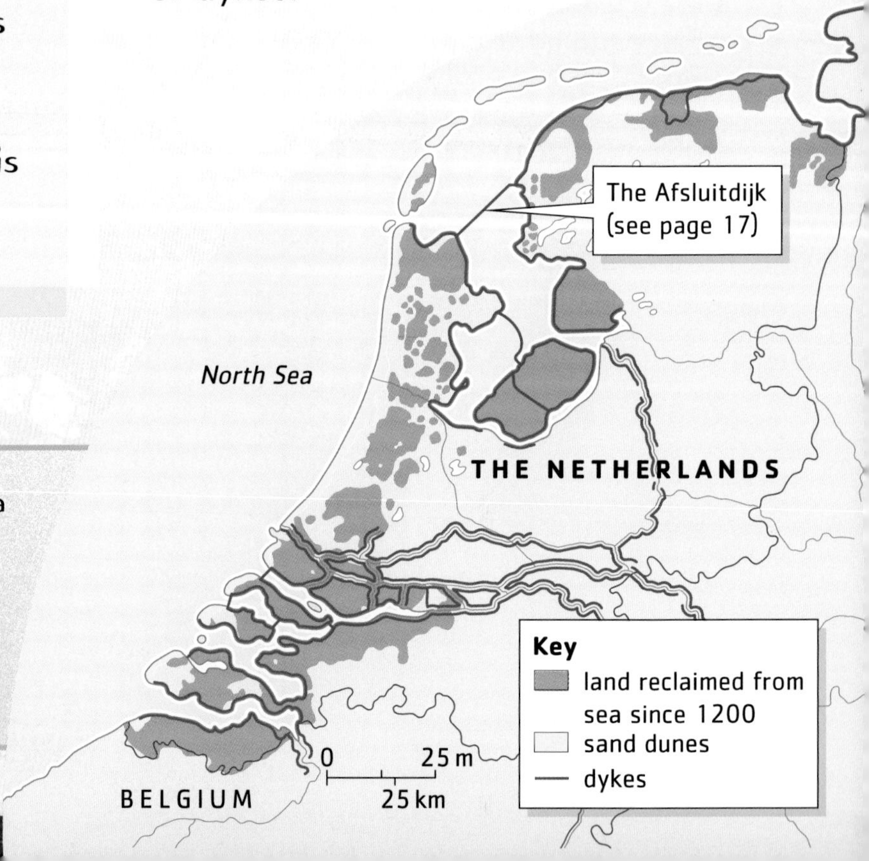

The Afsluitdijk (see page 17)
North Sea
THE NETHERLANDS
BELGIUM
0
25 m
25 km
Key
land reclaimed from sea since 1200
sand dunes
dykes

The Dutch have reclaimed a huge area of land from the sea. Today, low-lying areas are protected by a series of sand dunes and dykes.

CASE STUDY:
The Afsluitdijk, The Netherlands

Afsluitdijk is a Dutch word meaning 'enclosing **dam**'. It is a bank of soil in the Netherlands that stretches for 30 kilometres (19 miles) across an **inlet** of the North Sea. It was completed in 1933 after 6 years' work by 5000 people. Since then, a lot of the land behind the dam has been drained and **reclaimed** from the sea.

The dam was built from a material called till, a type of clay, held together with 18 million bundles of brushwood. Its slopes are covered with blocks of rock, to stop the clay being washed away. Grass on the top helps to bind it together and stop it being **eroded** by wind and rain. It is so wide that a road and cycle path have been built on top of it.

The Afsluitdijk is strong enough to hold back the power of the North Sea.

Why is soil important to scientists?

Scientists can learn more about the Earth, our history and also more recent events by studying soil. The mixture of materials in soil gives clues about the natural processes that shape the Earth. Soil may contain ash from an ancient **volcano**, **silt** from a flood long ago or burnt **particles** from a great fire.

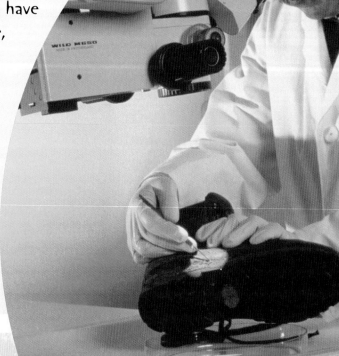

Soil on shoes or tyres can prove where a person has been recently.

Did you know?

Soil can help to solve crimes. When you walk across a muddy field, some of the mud sticks to your shoes. It shows where you have been. After a serious crime, any soil found on people's clothes or car tyres is collected and studied by scientists. The materials, seeds and **organisms** it contains may prove where someone has walked or driven. It may link them to the crime.

What does soil tell us about the past?

Digging down through soil is like travelling back in time. Scientists who try to understand the past by digging into the ground are called archaeologists. They scrape away the soil, layer by layer, and find parts of old buildings, everyday objects and even skeletons from long ago. The deeper they dig, the older the things they find are. Some things they look for are difficult to see and very easily destroyed. Dark stains in the soil may show where wooden posts that held up a building thousands of years ago stood. Blackened soil may show where a fire was made and food cooked. If the soil is washed away or dug out, this important information about our past could be lost forever.

Soil may contain clues to events long ago, such as bush fires.

How does soil move around?

Soil is moved great distances by the forces of nature. For example, dry soil can be whipped up into the air by the wind. The smallest **particles** take a long time to fall back to the ground. Sunlight passing through them may change colour, producing colourful sunsets.

Rivers can move large amounts of soil hundreds of kilometres.

Soil can also be moved by **landslides** and water. If soil is washed into rivers, it quickly separates into its different parts. Sandy particles fall to the bottom and plant material floats on top. You can see this if you put some soil in a bottle of water, shake it up and leave it to stand. The sand, grit and plant material in soil can be carried a long way by rivers or sea currents before they reach land again. There, they may help to form new soil.

How do people move soil?

Soil is transported by trucks. When new homes are built, new soil is brought in to create the gardens. It is spread on the ground so that grass and other plants will grow well.

Trucks like this one can tip their load of soil where it is needed.

CASE STUDY:
The Canterbury Plains, New Zealand

The Canterbury Plains are a vast flat area of land on New Zealand's South Island. The plains are the result of about two million years of soil and **gravel** being moved by nature from one place to another.

Glaciers and rivers flowing down from the mountains of the Southern Alps carried gravel and fine **silt** down with them. In time, the silt became so deep that it covered all the hills and valleys of the ground below. The rivers spread out across the flattened land, dropping more and more **sediment**. Today, the sediments that form the Canterbury Plains are more than 150 metres (490 feet) deep in places.

The soil that covers New Zealand's Canterbury Plains was brought down from the Southern Alps mountain range by rivers.

How can soil be harmed?

Soil can be harmed in many ways. Some of the damage is done by nature and some is done by people.

A long period of drought (a spell without rain) can dry out soil so much that wind can blow it away. Heavy rain can wash soil away too. Losing soil by wind or water is called **erosion**. When people cut down trees or clear land for farming, the soil is no longer held together by the roots of plants. This makes soil erosion more likely.

Many of the chemicals used in industry are harmful to soil. In the past, some industries poured their waste chemicals into the ground. Sometimes, dangerous chemicals were buried in the ground to get rid of them, but their containers leaked and the soil was polluted. Many plants and creatures that live in soil are killed by pollution. Some plants grow and take up the pollution through their roots. People and other animals who eat plants from polluted soil can become very ill.

Soil is at most risk of erosion when it is bare.

How can watering the ground harm soil?

In places where the land is too dry to grow crops, extra water is sometimes supplied by wells or pipelines. Watering land for agriculture is called irrigation. Irrigation water contains a tiny amount of salt. Over a long time, the salt can build up in the soil. However, most plants and **organisms** cannot live in salty soil. Salt pollution is a serious problem in places such as Pakistan, where irrigation is essential for farming.

Rain running through polluted soil can carry the pollution into nearby rivers.

How do farmers look after soil?

In nature, the **nutrients** and **organic** matter in soil are constantly **recycled**. They are used by plants and animals, and returned to the soil when plants die and as manure (dung) from animals. On a farm, nutrients and organic matter are taken away every time crops are harvested, so they have to be replaced. Farmers work **fertilizer** and manure into the soil. However, some of the fertilizers and other chemicals used on farms can be washed off the land by rain into **reservoirs** and rivers where people's drinking water comes from.

Do organic farmers look after soil differently?

Organic farmers are farmers who use as few chemicals as possible. Their aim is to keep their soil as natural as possible, so that safer and healthier food can be produced.

Organic farmers let hedges and wild plants grow around their fields to reduce soil **erosion** and provide **habitats** for creatures that control pests. These vegetables have been mixed with French marigolds.

How does soil affect the way we live?

Soil affects our lives in many ways. It is at the heart of most of the world's food production. Buildings, roads and bridges are built on it. Many of the materials our homes are built from depend on soil or materials that are grown in soil, such as wood.

How does soil affect buildings?

If soil dries out quickly, it can sink, or subside. If it soaks up a lot of extra water quickly, it can swell up, or heave. Subsidence and heave can move the ground enough to damage buildings. It is important for builders to understand what the ground is like before they start building on it.

If the ground dries out or swells up with water, it can move enough to crack a building's walls.

CASE STUDY:
The Leaning Tower of Pisa, Italy

The Leaning Tower of Pisa, in Italy, is one of the world's most famous buildings. It leans because it was built on soft ground. Soon after building work began in 1173, it started sinking, but it sank more on one side.

By 1990, it was about to collapse. Heavy lead bars were piled up on one side to squash the ground and stop the tower from leaning any more. In 1999, holes were drilled into the ground on one side of the tower and soil was pulled out. The holes made the tower sink on one side, tilting it back and saving it from collapse.

The famous Leaning Tower of Pisa leans because it has sunk into the ground unevenly.

What happens to soil during an earthquake?

An **earthquake** can crack the ground open and bring buildings tumbling down. It can also affect soil in a very strange way. When soil containing a lot of sand and water is shaken by an earthquake, it can behave like a liquid! It flows like water. Heavy things on top of it, including buildings, can sink into it. This is called liquefaction.

What are soil's hidden dangers?

Dangers can lurk unseen underneath soil. In places where there was a lot of **mining** in the past, long-forgotten mine shafts (tunnels) can collapse without warning, leaving a large hole in a road or in someone's garden! In places where wars

Natural forces sometimes move soil to where it is not wanted.

have been fought, landmines (bombs hidden in the soil) still remain. Many people are injured and crippled by stepping on landmines laid during recent wars in eastern Europe and Africa. Bombs that were dropped 60 years ago, during the Second World War, are also still found from time to time.

CASE STUDY:
The American Dust Bowl, USA

The lives of thousands of people in the USA were affected by a change in their soil. In the 1930s, a huge area of US farmland changed from growing grass to growing wheat. Unfortunately, soon after the grass was ploughed up, the worst drought in US history began. Without roots, **organic** matter or water to hold the soil together, it quickly dried out and strong winds began blowing it away. More than 865 million tonnes of soil was blown off the land in only one year (1935).

The soil became so poor that nothing would grow in it. Farmers were unable to make a living from the land and they left in their thousands to look for work elsewhere. Rain finally returned and ended the drought in 1939.

A drought in the 1930s changed much of the farm soil in the USA into dust.

Will soil ever run out?

Soil will not run out, because new soil is constantly being made and **recycled** in nature. Although soil will not run out, it is not always in the place where it is needed most. Wind and water can move it away from farmland.

How can we look after soil?

Soil has to be in good condition with plenty of **nutrients** and **organic** matter to grow healthy crops, so we need to take good care of soil that is used to produce food. Organic food production keeps soil in the most natural condition. Pollution can undo all this good work and damage soil, so we must also protect the land from pollution.

Using organic farming methods, like allowing ladybirds to eat unwanted pests rather than killing them with chemicals, is one way of protecting soil from pollution.

Glossary

dam bank of soil or a concrete wall built across a river to hold back the water

earthquake a violent shaking of the ground

erosion slow removal of soil by wind or water

fertile having all the nutrients and organic matter necessary to produce healthy plant growth

fertilizer substance that is used to make soil more fertile

fungi plants (including mushrooms and toadstools) that get the food they need by taking it from other plants or from dead plant material

glacier very slow-moving river of ice that flows down the side of a mountain

gravel mixture of small pebbles and pieces of rock larger than about 2 millimetres across

habitat place where plants and animals normally live

humus dead and partly rotted parts of plants found in soil

inlet bay or opening in a coastline

landslide a fall of soil and rock down the side of a hill or mountain. Also called a landslip.

limestone type of white rock made mainly from chalk and often containing millions of skeletons of tiny sea creatures

litter zone surface of soil, covered with dead leaves and twigs

microbes tiny organisms, so small that they can only be seen by looking through a microscope

mining digging into the ground to reach valuable materials such as coal

nutrients chemicals used by plants and animals to help them grow

organic material from plants and animals, alive or dead. All the material in soil that is alive or was once alive is organic. The sand, clay and silt in soil are not organic, because they were never alive.

organisms living plants or animals, including bacteria, algae and worms. The smallest plants and animals are also called micro-organisms.

particle tiny piece

reclaim change a shallow part of the sea into dry land by building banks of soil and blocks of stone or concrete around it and taking the water out

recycling using materials more than once

reservoir human-made lake that supplies water to people's homes

rock-fall a pile of rocks slipping down a hillside or mountainside

sediment material, such as silt, that settles to the bottom of water

silt very fine particles of rock just a fraction of a millimetre across – less than the size of a full stop on this page. Silt is found in rivers and the sea.

volcano hole in the Earth's crust where lava comes out. The lava often builds up to form a mountain.

Find out more

Books

Rocks and Minerals: Soil, Melissa Stewart (Heinemann Library, 2002)

Rocks, Minerals and Soil, B. J. Knapp (Atlantic Europe Publishing Co, 2001)

Websites

www.school.discovery.com/schooladventures/soil
Information about soil from the Discovery Channel.

www.blm.gov/nstc/soil/Kids
Amazing facts about soil from the US National Science & Technology Centre Bureau of Land Management.

www.waite.adelaide.edu.au/school/Soil/
Soil, how it is formed, what it contains and how it can be harmed, from the University of Adelaide in Australia.

www.epa.gov/superfund/students/wastsite/soilspil.htm
Information about soil contamination (pollution), from the US Environmental Protection Agency.

www.landcare.gov.au
Information about looking after the land, from the Australian government's Department of Agriculture, Fisheries and Forestry.

Index

Titles in the *Earth's Precious Resources* series include:

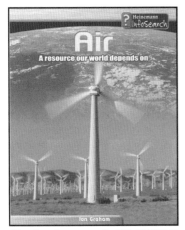

Hardback   0 431 11556 7

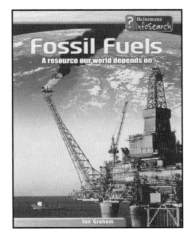

Hardback   0 431 11550 8

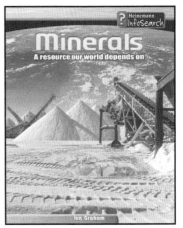

Hardback   0 431 11552 4

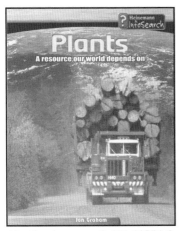

Hardback   0 431 11551 6

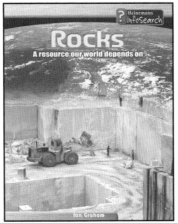

Hardback   0 431 11553 2

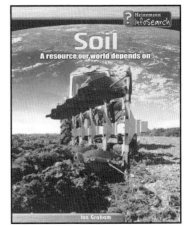

Hardback   0 431 11554 0

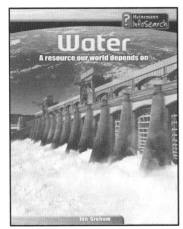

Hardback   0 431 11555 9

Find out about the other titles in this series on our website www.heinemann.co.uk/library